# Happily Ever Always™

*A Top-Selling Real Estate Broker's Secret Guide to Confidence, Contentedness and Security*

# Michael Rosenblum

**TRADECRAFT**

Tradecraft Books, Los Angeles 90046

©2018 by Tradecraft Books

All rights reserved. Published 2018

Printed in the United States of America

ISBN: 978-0-9981693-9-2

Rosenblum, Michael

Happily Ever Always™

A Top-Selling Real Estate Broker's Secret Guide to

Confidence, Contentedness and Security

Book cover and interior design: Kevin Corcoran Jr.

Author photo: Aubrey Navarro / Bleederhead Studio

To Stephen – you inspire me in more ways than
you imagine

To Marilyn – you are my star

To Marvin – forever my mentor

To Bernice – my greatest spiritual teacher

# Table of Contents

"What lies before us and what lies behind us are tiny matters compared to what lies within us."
– Ralph Waldo Emerson

# Foreword

Molly and I met Michael as most people meet him—through a friend. One day there was a phone call, "I know this guy, you've got to meet him." The next day he was in our office talking about life and people and cracking wise. The next thing we knew, he was shaping how we viewed the world.

Having known him for years now, we know his friendships last forever. We know he believes fervently in everything he says. And we know more than anything that he follows through on his word. We've met a lot of people in our careers in marketing, advertising, and public relations. We've met celebrities, experts and savants. But we've never met anyone quite like Michael.

As the concept for his book grew and evolved, we knew it was important for him to meet as many people as he could... perhaps more than he can touch simply through his real estate business, because his message is easy to digest and important in uncertain times.

With the context now to look back on the writing he has done here, it's more evident than ever that this isn't just a book about being a better real estate agent or how to buy a house more confidently... though you could certainly lift that message.

This is a book about pulling the lessons from life, living consciously, and creating an outcome that you are ultimately entitled to experience. Michael's process is life-long and his own trials and tribulations, outcomes and successes, bear observation and study. But more importantly, they bear participation.

He has created that opportunity here, to learn from his own experiences at least as a method for looking within yourself. Then to write down your own experiences and later to reflect and synthesize. As you make your way through his journey—and yours—

you'll find yourself writing a book of your own, so to speak.

And that's perhaps what we find most inspiring here. We all have a book of challenges, lessons, and learnings within us. Someone who can help reveal that within ourselves is important to all of us. Michael certainly has been incredibly important to both of us as we've made our choices at critical junctures in our own lives.

We suspect the same will be true for you.

--Jim Jacoby and Molly Morter, June 2017

# An Introduction

Are you happy? Do you accept yourself? Have you ever taken the time to learn who you are, why you are here? Have you discovered your personal truth?

I was that kid who felt different growing up, bullied at times, feeling like I really didn't fit in, wondering why I was me. And at times, wanting to be someone else.

As time passed and events (even the unpleasant ones) became part of my history, I began to realize that these experiences were something to be cherished. That I had a purpose for being on this planet and I was actually okay. That acceptance slowly evolved into a kind of pride in who I was, what I had survived and that I deserved good things in life – deserved to be happy.

Like many people I equated professional achievement (and money) with happiness, and for me, happiness was really about security. But what I came to find was that financial security didn't necessarily make me happy, it was the "emotional" security that I so desperately sought. This began the journey to find out if such a thing was possible, and if so, how.

Ultimately, my travels around the globe taught me while there are many differences among cultures there are more similarities among humankind. One of the most universal emotions is love – giving it, finding it usually get top billing but what about loving yourself? Not being a narcissist, but accepting oneself in a pure, authentic and healthy way.

For me, the first step was to own my unique self and when I began to love me, well, that is when I found the emotional security that has grounded my professional success. I own the "pieces" to my puzzle and finally understand how they fit together.

Your path to this self-acceptance will be different from mine. But I hope parts of my story resonate with you and perhaps open up a way to find your own emotional security and happiness.

I'm not a psychologist, and don't pretend to have all of life's answers. I only share what has worked (and not worked) for me to find the intersection between peace and prosperity.

That being said, please approach this book as a process. It's meant to be organic and reflective.

When you are finished, I truly hope you will find the emotional security you rightfully deserve.

Keep in mind, that the weather patterns of life are unpredictable and the only key to finding my security has been learning to love myself.

I wish the same for you. Let's begin!

# 1.0
# Self-Understanding

I t might sound a little strange, but I ask myself from time to time, "Who is Michael Rosenblum?" To some, I may be a top-selling real estate broker, or partner, son, friend, uncle, healer. But these are only adjectives that describe me, not define me. I define myself, through my daily interactions. How I treat others is really who I am.

In short, Michael Rosenblum is me and I have always been he, constantly evolving.

As I get older, the adjectives may change but the core of who I am remains constant. And so, the challenges of my own journey create a wider kaleidoscope of who I am becoming.

This understanding has created a personal peace and a level of professional success I would like to share. But first, let me explain what peace and success mean to me. For me, learning to love myself has been the gift of peace. Accepting my flaws and faults; learning to make lemonade from my own lemons has been my pathway to success. People often equate my success to some outside source such as money or love, but, in reality success is merely an accomplishment and doesn't sustain my own security of peace. I have lost money and I have fallen out of love. I have learned by loving, trusting and valuing myself I become empowered to achieve success through the security of peace.

However, coming to this sort of peace is a process and evolving successfully in business and relationships is challenging. As I've gained greater success in my career, I've taken more and more careful note of just how these changes happen.

In this book, I'll share my process with you. I'm excited about it. In fact, when we meet, you'll find that I'm overjoyed by it. I'm excited because I can connect with even more amazing people in entirely new ways ... and I know learning from one another we can make each of our experiences even more remarkable than they already are.

Our path together will be an ongoing journey which starts with ourselves. We build individual intentions.   Everyone is born with special gifts I call "tools". These tools help navigate us. We build momentum. We present ourselves. And we learn how others perceive us.

I am a lifelong entrepreneur, having pioneered media companies and magazines, eventually becoming a top 1% producing broker and a major player in a top-tier real estate market.

Business is what I know, and through business, I have come to understand myself. Ask yourself who *you* are as we share our stories with each other. I've created spaces in this book to include your own reflections and experiences along the way. As we progress, I'll share my own stories in the spirit of vulnerability and inspiration. Respectfully, I ask you to reflect on your own life without judgment.

I believe that together we can find the truth that is right for you, live into that truth more actively, and improve the circumstances in our lives... from personal to business and everywhere in between.

# 1.1

# On Becoming

My mother and father—Marilyn and Marvin: my star and mentor, respectively— taught me commitment to the things that matter. This fundamental lesson has made me who I am today. Every coworker and client passing through my office over the years also brought lessons – grand or small. I believe the universe brings these lessons to our doorsteps in novel ways. It's up to us to learn how to see them.

Personal truth is the security you find when you eventually learn to love yourself. My personal truth has taught me that life folds back on itself – that truth evolves over time and not at a consistent speed. It's like a bird that drops a seed from the fruit of the tree which germinates, yet again, to become a new tree, made stronger by the decisions we've made and the people to whom we've tied our stories. I've also learned that when you let others stabilize themselves on your own foundations, you gain far more down the road. Nurturing another person to awaken the gifts you see sleeping within them tie you to the people and things that make your true self flourish and they will help to raise you higher than you could imagine.

Relationships are not created between two people, but stem from a beautifully tangled web of connections we trace between each other and the world around us. I was lucky to have support from my parents encouraging me to go after my dreams. After college, I relied on others who came before me to help me establish myself. For example, I cold called to get informational interviews always hoping to connect with others. And it worked. They all helped me find my gifts that made me successful. My career didn't come without challenges.

When business associates or partner companies attempted to take advantage of me or cut me out of the picture altogether, I held my ground. My career did not come without challenges. I faced lawsuits head on rather than being a doormat to those who would bully or attempt to deceive me. At least once I found myself financially broke, rebuilding my wealth as a result. I've learned that failure is only a mask to success when you challenge yourself.

Through all of the trials and triumphs, one thing has never changed — my word has always been my bond and I apply myself fully to my commitments. My word and truth are the core of my soul and have been since birth. When I tell somebody that I will do something or that I can do something or that I will do something, *I do it.*

No matter what it takes. No matter how long it takes. No matter what it costs; I do it.

If you put this book down right now and never pick it back up again, if you remember only one thing from these pages, let it be that a commitment to *your word* is something every person deserves. Expect nothing less and give nothing less and you'll live your happily ever after—always.

Today, my chosen joy is making home ownership a reality for people from all walks of life. I do everything I can to help minimize the anxiety of every little detail. It's where I've come to feel fulfilled in what I do, while also utilizing things I'm good at. You could say I'm happy.

But happiness isn't a state of mind, or a moment: it's a journey we have only just begun.

# 1.2

# **Discovering Gifts**

I believe we were all born with gifts. Some of us are natural artists. Some of us are endowed with an incredible enthusiasm for numbers. There are also more discrete gifts—what we bring to the experiences of others. My mother, for example, is possessed of incredible strength which she passes on to those who meet her. My father, was an unconditional giver and motivator, augmenting his wife's gifts. Together, they taught me some of the foundational lessons of my childhood. By cutting away the chains that bonded them with very challenging childhoods.

For most people, uncovering gifts is a process. There are people who say, "I'm not good at anything." We're not all lucky enough to have encouraging parents but what we lack in one area, we often make up in another. Like a deck of playing cards, everyone has a joker. But the beauty is you're able to reshuffle, which allows you to find your ace! You discover your gifts by trying out different things and not being afraid to fail. You learn that failure is only success trying to be reborn in a better way. You realize fear is faith turned inside out. And, by wrapping yourself in the blanket of faith you find comfort through the discovery by gifts.

At varying times in our lives, we discover new interests, new loves and desires that drive us to success or failure. You leave some by the roadside, others you keep close for the duration of our journey, tending to and enhancing them with every subsequent experience. At some point, I've found my own gifts leading me to new and greater things—guiding me down paths I never imagined would be laid out before me.

I believe, eventually, these gifts become who we are, and give us the ability to discover our potential. Though naturally occurring within us, they are not always apparent. We spend a lot of time *not* knowing where we are meant to end up. It's a circuitous path we stumble along, sometimes for a very long time — at least, that seems to be the case with most of us. We may have inklings of our greater purpose as we progress, but what lies ahead is ever shrouded in mystery until we choose to forge ahead and find out where we're going.

# Exercise Set 1:
# **Your Gift Guide**

Identify one or two of your gifts?

_____

_____

_____

How did you discover them?

_____

_____

_____

Were you supported in your gifts in your childhood
and beyond?

_____

_____

_____

By whom?

_____

_____

_____

If you weren't, how did that affect the development of your gifts?

_____

_____

_____

# 2.0
# **Discrete Gifts**

P erhaps you believe we are simply born, live, die and anything that happens to us along the way is just randomly ordered. Or perhaps you're more of a fatalist, believing that our destiny is predetermined and nothing we do (good or bad) will influence our future. I fall somewhere in between. I believe we are all assigned a destiny – but how (or if) we get there is really determined by us. The world asks us to change our plans and reorient ourselves almost constantly. This might appear random, but it isn't. The secret is to be aware of this and be ready.

Preparation + Opportunity = Luck.

Have you ever been pulled in one direction or another? How about a voice that nags you to do this, not that? What's happened when you've ignored that feeling or that voice? My guess is that things didn't go too well. I follow that inner voice because it's never steered me wrong.

However, it's not just your inner voice that can act as a guide. Look around. Everyone is on their own journey, but a lot of paths have similar experiences. When paths intersect a lesson can be learned, a message passed, if you're open to it. There are lessons everywhere, clues to how to move forward. Other people are also some of our most valuable assets if we allow them to be. They can offer us valuable feedback and insight into our own behavior. We might not want to hear it, but it will probably do us good. The key is to pay attention and listen. After all, we were born with two ears and one mouth, so we should listen twice as much as we talk.

## 2.1

# Activating Gifts

We're not always ready to share certain gifts with the world. And some of us wind up letting our dreams fall by the wayside. In my opinion, there is no wayside. When we move on to another dream, we are simply finding the way we were always meant to go. Voices of destiny can call us to different places at different times. There are always new mountains to climb.

Growing up, many kids want to be doctors or lawyers, many want to help people. What did you want to be? And why? From a very young age, I felt a special connection to animals, which made me seriously consider a veterinary career. My early observations of work were basically that people did what they really liked to do. It seemed like if you were passionate enough, you could grow up to be involved with that kind of work. You were creating yourself and showing the world the fulfillment of your life's purpose through your work.

Pets were always part of our home, and some of the happiest moments of my childhood were spent learning how to care for them properly. Melanie was my gerbil, Charlie was my chameleon, Muffin was my dog and like humans, animals hold us accountable to our word, even though the lines of communication can be slightly subtler. You commit to walking a dog every day, changing your cat's litter, cleaning the fish tank, and keeping the growing zoo in your home happy and well fed.

As I grew, I discovered other interests that tended to be centered around an entrepreneurial feeling brewing somewhere deep inside me. From my childhood home in Potomac, Maryland, I learned how to make candles and terrariums. I sold them around the neighborhood and found I reaped great joy from the work. Something about creating a product someone else found value in was attractive to me.

My father taught me how to work hard and always held me to the same standard he held for himself. Dad always followed through on his commitments and I learned, from a very young age, to wrap his philosophy into my own. I established a positive rapport with my customers and they brought more business my way through referrals. Everything I did came with a guarantee of satisfaction. In reflection, I believe these guarantees have led to my greatest successes.

I continued to tend this entrepreneurial attitude whether mowing lawns or shoveling snow. I learned the value of a job well done, the feeling of being trusted to complete a task on time and well done. Many people have had similar experiences growing up. But that only makes me more confident in the universality of my belief that anyone can find success rooted in these simple understandings.

# Exercise Set 2:
# **Self-Understanding**

This exercise is designed to challenge you to genuinely stop, reflect, and think deeply about who you really are. Take the time. Don't rush through your answers. These are your foundation. And, if after completing a couple further exercises you find that this exercise bears updating... just do it. Your constant unfolding requires constant reflection.

First, describe yourself in three sentences.

_____

_____

_____

Describe yourself as a family member would describe you.

_____

_____

_____

List your earliest passions and hobbies.

_____

_____

_____

List the jobs you believed you wanted to be when you
grew up.

_____

_____

_____

# 3.0
# **Your Word**

E ven when you seem to have nothing, you still have your word. And like any asset, your word has value—a value decided by the people to whom you give your word and your ability to follow through on the promises (spoken and unspoken) you make to the people around you. Fulfillment on your word compounds over time.

Even at a young age, I understood this to some degree. I always felt that I had to do an extra special job, so people wanted me to come back and help them again. It just seemed ingrained in my sense of being that if I performed well for people and made them happy that I would always be welcomed back to serve them again.

It was a different time, but the continuing importance of salespeople confirms the power of standing on a doorstep, fearlessly showing off your work and wares with the greatest pride. Sales, of course, have been a part of my life since childhood in some way or other. My relative success at door-to-door sales was an early cue the universe gave me, and it put me on a path of self-discovery I walk today.

In turn, I have many friends whose parents pushed them to study law and after many unhappy years in the field they have redirected their lives into other professions. Nothing is wasted. Recycling creates new usage. Skill sets are comported to another industry. Like my years in the media become a competitive edge for me to list and market homes. See, there are no mistakes and just like the navigation systems in our cars, if we get lost, if we make the wrong turn, we eventually get redirected to the path we are destined to journey, if we are open to listening to the voice we hear talking to us.

# 3.1
# Our Moments

I believe life and stories return to themselves, folding back on repeating themes. It's incredible how cyclical your life can be when examined through the right lens. When I encounter new situations or people, I like to reflect on the past. I look for associations between where I am today and where I was back when. I seek the differences, subtleties, and mistakes made in previous times.

When you're young, you have so many teachable moments. Stupid mistakes. Friends you wish you held onto. Some mistakes, you find out, turn out not to be mistakes at all. Some friends, you discover, were mistakes. Mistake or not, each moment and acquaintance is a lesson—a gift given to you by the Universe. When you learn to listen to those faint whispers of destiny, you bring yourself closer to realizing it.

A moment that often strikes a chord with me happened when I was very small—maybe as young as seven. I had climbed a tree in the wooded lot around my parents' home in Rockville, Maryland. While climbing, I took an unfortunate misstep, falling to the ground and scraping my knee. I got up and started again. Failure is success being reborn. I was determined to climb that tree. Eventually, my mother placed a bandage on my knee before going in for dinner.

Later that evening, I took a bath. As I soaked, I felt the bandage lift and sway as it slowly separated from my skin. Eventually, it was floating freely in the water. I picked up the bandage and my mind wandered. I thought very hard about the process of bandage making, the disparate materials gathered so that their traits might be combined into one useful tool.

I began to see that people weren't all that different from the bandage: so, ordinary and expected, yet complex and unique. Unknowingly, I had been thinking about reincarnation at that point in my life, and I wondered if I might return, in the next life, as a bandage or a strand of cotton woven into one. Maybe I would be a tree or an animal, a bird perhaps! It was then that I also imagined circumstances that would cause me to not come back after death to live again. What if the tree is cut? What if the cotton strand is engulfed in flame?

Eventually, I concluded that I would be myself for the time being. It's worked out so far and has made me a loyal supporter of my truest self: the self who questions the world that surrounds us all; the curious explorer and discoverer of new worlds hidden in the backyard; the tenacious man who makes his own way.

When I finally exited the tub, I was covered in wrinkles. My childhood thoughts in the tub may not seem revelatory, but it has only been in retrospect that I have come to view this moment as a subtle message from the Universe. Life awakened a curiosity within me, a higher concept entrenched in the pain of my scraped leg.

I still struggle to grasp the objective meaning of this moment, but subjectively it has applied itself to many situations throughout my life and career. Like a gemstone turning under a light, the crystalized form of a memory reflects new meanings when viewed from a different angle. For example, meeting a new associate, I wonder what they might have lived like in a past life. I think about how past lives are not only vague and impervious to direct examination while we live, but also while we exist within each current life.

Change may be the most constant gift the Universe has to offer. For better or worse, we can rely on our tomorrows to be distinct from today. As I journey through life, events become history and I chose to accept my defeats and victories, understanding that these moments will propel me toward further greatness. If I can't accept my defeats and I try to seek harbor in my victories I will not reach my potential.

This ribbon of my truth has been tested repeatedly, but I still believe in myself when people tell me I can't. I still know faith is just a practiced belief and the belief I practice can shape my dreams into reality. No matter how anxious, scared or nervous I might become on the road, my faith and positivity help turn fear inside out to reveal new strength. No matter

how alone I feel in hard times, I am comforted
knowing that I will never give up.

# Exercise Set 3:
# **Choosing to Be**

This exercise is designed to focus on the choices you make as you become more aware of the decisions available to you and the reflections those may reveal in and of themselves.

First, have you ever felt as if the Universe was sending you a message? What happened?

_____

_____

_____

Think back to a major decision you have had to make. What did you decide and why?

_____

_____

_____

What made your choice "correct" for you?

_____

_____

_____

Think about another choice that you have regretted.
What made you realize the decision was not the correct
one for you?

_____

_____

_____

The exercise you just completed is great – but what if
we don't know how to listen to how the universe is
helping you? How does one do this? Listening to the
universe is not putting on your headphones and tuning
into some other voice. It is listening to your own gut,
losing the emotion, trusting your soul to direct you on
your path paved with or without rocks. And about
rocks; diamonds are rocks which endure the roughest
cut and polish to shine the brightest and be worth the
most.  Are we any different?

# 4.0

# **Learning by Doing**

I t is important that we not become complacent. When we stand still, we cease to grow. We become comfortable with our stature, but the next level is still out there if only we had the strength to reach it. In the continuum of experiences that shape us into the people we become, it is our responsibility to be aware. It is when we know the meaning of our experiences that we become self-aware. This is the only way we truly learn how to do anything in life.

To learn, you must do. And to do your best, you must think and pause and reflect and never, ever, stop.

It may be a tired metaphor to say we are all laboratory concoctions, yet it remains relevant to how we are continually reacting with the world around us—testing our substance against new challenges. Each of our chemistries produces different results when mixed into a new situation or with a new person. The summation of subtle choices accumulates, and we become a new compound.

We learn, slowly, with each test, the ability to modify our behaviors. We discover which results move us closer to our goals and desires. In this way, we become who we want—fashioning our lives with every decision. If a choice doesn't work, we can modify our behaviors—redirecting our focus toward a new destiny. And if we maintain our faith and positivity, we will eventually succeed.

Put simply, we must act in the present, reflecting on the past, to improve the future. Through acting, analyzing, and reflecting, everyone gains the ability to achieve their proper destiny. This isn't a new model or method, but it is one we might not give as much credit to.

Another moment from my past I like to reflect on is my first night at the University of Missouri.

I didn't know a soul. I was uncomfortable and anxious. I wasn't the only one. My roommate put the moment into context when he said, ""You can make a bad situation good, or a good situation bad."

A light bulb went off in my head—how true. From there, I knew I had to be in ultimate control of my life. I would be responsible for my actions and outcomes entirely. Those poignant words, at such a transformative moment in my life, enmeshed themselves into the fabric of my personal truth. I put them into practice, and let my undergraduate experience begin.

By the time I had graduated with a degree in Business Administration, I realized I had been directing myself towards a career in the business of media. It seemed perfectly natural. My entire life had folded in on itself in the best possible way; all my interests and experiences had added up to this moment. I liked the Midwest, so I stayed, eventually moving to Chicago, ready to create the life I wanted. But I was after more than material success and gratification. Yes, those were certainly goals, but there was a higher one. Like a lot of young people, fresh out of college, I wanted to change the world. It was quite a tall and idealistic order, and little did I know it how much time it would take and how many lessons I had to learn to have any kind of positive impact on others.

## 4.1
# Destiny's Author

I have often thought that life has an uncanny resemblance to a stage play. I'm certainly not the first person to apply the metaphor but it's one that has helped me organize my own thoughts about personal destiny. So, with all deference to those who've made the comparison, including the great William Shakespeare whose Macbeth laments about the "poor player" who "struts and frets his hour upon the stage," I humbly submit my own observations and conclusions.

For starters, there's an opening act and an ending act, and acts in between. Just how many acts we have can be vastly different from person to person. One person may have 12 acts and another just three, as everyone is on a different path. However, how we strut confidentially or fret miserably during them is ultimately up to each of us.

Like a play, characters will come in and out of our lives. Some may be simply walk-ons and cameos, while others will surround us through a significant part of our lives, acting as leads. Of course, every compelling play has conflict. Your life has its share, I'm certain. The conflict, or "drama" is driven by protagonists (heroes) and antagonists (villains). Think of who these characters were in your past and present? The point is, a play needs conflict which requires both heroes and villains. And guess what? You need them in life, too. As you're very aware, not all lessons are taught through the generosity of loved ones or the kindness of strangers. Some of the toughest are learned through dealings with people who seek to do us harm by manipulation and sabotage. Here's where I'm going to ask you to envision your life without any villains. At first, it might seem like a good idea. However, if not all inspiration comes from good things, without villains, where would you be? Perhaps a villain in your childhood motivated you to be bigger, faster and stronger on the football field? Or, maybe the villain in your office pushed you to work harder. Don't wish your villains away; they are some of your best teachers. Forgive them and their trespasses because, after all, they were only playing a critical role in your personal and professional development. Next, pay attention to the plot points in your life. In other words, are the plot points moving your story forward, backward or in a circle? In real-world terms, this could mean dating the same type of person again and again, each time with the relationship imploding. Or it could be staying in a dead-end job because you're too scared or lazy to find something more promising and fulfilling.

If this sounds like you (even a little), you're hardly alone. The truth is, most of us are slaves to our habits and routines. However, if your patterns are keeping you in perpetual limbo, it's time to act. Think of it as watching the first act of a play in a loop, without ever getting to the second act? Sounds like a bore. In the same respect, if your life is stuck in the opening act, you risk the same thing – boredom and stagnation. Playing your life in a loop prevents you from advancing and maturing, and certainly not reaching your full potential. In the end, no matter how many acts we stage in our life, there will come a time for the final curtain.

# Exercise Set 4:
# **Acting the Part**

What will your reviews say about your performance?

_____

_____

_____


Which "act" do you think you're in right now? Why?

_____

_____

_____


Do you believe you should be in another act?

_____

_____

_____


Identify one protagonist (hero) in your life. They can be from the past or present. What makes them a hero?

_____

_____

_____

What was the most important lesson you learned from them?

_____

_____

_____

Now, name an antagonist from your life (past or present). What makes them a villain? What have you learned about yourself from their actions?

_____

_____

_____

Be honest, what are some patterns or habits in your life you believe have held you back either personally or professionally, or both?   Do you want to break them? Have you tried?

_____

_____

_____

## 5.0
# Starting Where You Are

Every play needs a setting, and, after college, I found mine. I chose Chicago because I liked the Midwestern attitude I had discovered in college. I found myself a cheap apartment and, after a short search, I was steadily employed as a waiter at the Marriott Hotel on Michigan Avenue.

I had worked in a restaurant as a dishwasher when I was 16. Back then, while washing dishes, I saw a woman pushing a cart, tending to what they called the salad bar back in the '70s. I thought, "Oh, that looks like an interesting position. I love salads so why not do that?"

I asked the managers if I could switch roles. They weren't hiring anyone for that position, but they liked me, so they let me do it anyway. Charm is magic: remember that. I got out of dishwashing, but it made me sensitive to dishwashers. It's not the most interesting work. If you're a thinker, like myself, maybe it's fine. Complacency is also fine for some people, but not for me. Dishwashers do perform a valuable service and deserve our respect.

While working the salad bar, I noticed people leaving money on tables after sitting there.
I thought, "Oh my god. I could be a server. It's like being an actor."

I've always thought I would have been a decent actor. No matter what I do, I use a similar skill set. If I'm selling real estate, or jeans, whether I'm selling advertising for a magazine, or air time on a television station—it's a lot like being an actor in a show.

You must rely on your salesmanship, humor, sensitivities, charm and intuition. It's translating a skill set and experiences of your life to be successful. It's simply a matter of getting outside yourself from time to time and managing your own 'ins and outs' as an actor would inhabit a persona.

The restaurant only had female servers, but I charmed them into hiring me to mix it up a little. I started waiting tables and I made amazing money. Sometimes I would make $100 in an eight-hour shift (which would be well over $300 in today's dollars.)

Thankfully, it went well. Before long, customers were requesting to sit in my section. Management took notice and I was promoted to head waiter. This actually surprised me because post-college, the Marriott where I worked had some hardcore service industry folks. These were the real pros. My manager was tough, and I never thought she liked me very much. She pegged me as some college kid trying to make a name for himself. She wasn't wrong, but I felt like I had a target on my back most of the time.

Although I was good at my server job, my eye was always on getting into the business end of media. So, with every free moment, I worked the pavement, cold-calling every magazine office in the city. It was tricky. I wanted them to hire me, but I also wanted them to teach me how to sell advertising space. Not many employers want to pay you to learn on the job, but I didn't give up.

I'm not sure how many informational meetings and interviews I went on, but it was a lot. Ultimately, however, all the legwork paid off. I landed a job and all the people I encountered on my journey became the foundation for my professional network – one that continues to benefit me to this day.

# 5.1
# Your Inner Voice

I got hired at News Voice Newspapers: a newspaper chain on the North Shore. I started by selling advertising door-to-door. Of course, I wasn't making much money back then, so I kept my restaurant job on the side.

I pursued my first media job with a vengeance. I would go into mom and pop stores in my territory and convince people to buy advertising. I met very interesting people. And, even though the work could be trying, I was determined to build a track record of proven experience—knowing that would help get me to the next step.

I had grand illusions, but I came to learn that I couldn't take the president's chair and work my way down: I had to start in the quicksand and work my way up. I really wanted to work for a fancy magazine, but I had to pay my dues.

I also had to keep paying my bills, so I kept working at the Marriott on the weekends to make ends meet, which meant working seven days a week. After about nine months, I felt ready to take the next step and began interviewing. In a relatively short period of time, I had learned a lot about media sales and ready to swim in a bigger pond.

# Exercise Set 5:
# **Reflections**

This exercise is designed to build a sense of understanding of those around you today and how you see yourself in light of those reflections. In particular, what are your strengths among friends and colleagues and acknowledging them for use in the future.

First, think about someone you admire. What makes them special?

_____

_____

_____

Do you think they have had times of feeling directionless? How would you picture them persevering?

_____

_____

_____

What do you have the most success with today, and
what makes you good in that area?

_____

_____

_____


What do you think others admire about you?

_____

_____

_____

## 6.0
# Your Calling

In time, I landed a position at an up-and-coming magazine downtown—a local publication. The magazine's owner saw something in me and gave me the opportunity to prove my potential. I didn't let her down. In my first month, I sold more than anybody else on staff. The next month, I sold even more. I continued to do so, month after month, for several years.

The magazine was doing well, and advertising sales were better than ever. Eventually, I told my manager at the Marriott that I was quitting. I'll never forget her reaction. She told me I should keep working for her in case I got fired. She played the villain in my last restaurant scene. I wasn't mad, I was motivated. I thanked her and quit anyway.

At the magazine, I continued to grow my book of sales and eventually, I was asked to become the advertising director of the magazine. Everyone there was astonished at what I was producing. My track record was way beyond anyone else on staff.

I thought to myself, "This is it." I knew I could do this sales thing. It was where I belonged. I was exhilarated. I felt empowered. I felt accomplished. I felt incredible. I felt that I was on the path to great things. I had set a goal and I had accomplished my goal, but now there was so much more to be done.

I had to learn management skills on the job using my intuition. It was a lot of work to manage people and all the sales work. And there were plenty of people on staff who refused to accept someone younger than themselves as their boss. Eventually, I got the hang of it and was able to keep everyone on track.

I started to make the magazine a lot of money. Huge amounts of money. Me? I made $18,000 per year, plus commissions. But commissions were paid quarterly. It got to the point where I wanted to buy a condo, and I needed a little more stability with my monthly income. I had to ask my boss—appropriately—for more.

## 6.1
# Instinct

It is common knowledge that when someone says, "I'll think about it," they mean, "No." When I asked my boss for a raise or, at least a more regular commission structure, the boss said, "I'll think about it."

I remember the follow up conversation with my boss vividly. I was traveling, flying back from visiting my parents so my boss and I had planned to talk on the phone.

When I dialed her, I was pretty confident she'd offer me a raise. After all, I had delivered her record sales and was a loyal employee.

No dice. She said there would be no raise, no restructure, no nothing.

She said, "That's just how it has to be." "Well, actually it's not," I replied. "That's not going to work for me." She told me I didn't have a choice. But I did, and I told her I was quitting. No, I didn't have another job lined up and she knew it. My boss was shocked, and maybe I was a little too. But I said, "You don't need to worry about me. I'll give you my notice when I get back."

I hung up the phone and it hit me. I had listened to my instinct, but I did not listen to my wallet. I had credit card debt and bills with next to nothing in my savings account.

While I vexed over my decision in the airport, the universe sent me a sign. A friend-of-a-friend saw me at the gate by chance and said hello. She was a frequent flyer with the airline and asked if I wanted to sit with her in first class.

I said I couldn't really upgrade because I had just quit my job. She just laughed at me. All she had to do was use her airline status to request an empty seat. I flew back home in style with a new friend. I had never sat in first-class before. I knew then that a new adventure was waiting, just beyond the horizon.

## 6.2
# Direction

I knew I had made the right decision. In retrospect, I recognize that my chance meeting with my friend, getting upgraded to first class, and coming back to people supporting my decision were signs. I was heading in the right direction.

I felt really good and comfortable about what I had done. I was at peace with my ambitions for the moment.

Nobody wanted to hire me while I was still at the magazine, but as soon as I gave my notice, I received several enticing offers. I needed to control my life rather than allowing someone else to.

After it was confirmed that I was leaving, a rival magazine called me and inquired about hiring me. Instinctively I asked, "Why don't we just do it on a consulting basis. I really don't want to necessarily work for a company right now."

The magazine was called *Inside Chicago*. It was like *Chicago Magazine*. I had gotten him a few clients, and, in a few days, I made $5,000 in commissions. Then one of my advertisers at the prior magazine connected me to a firm called Churchill, Sterling & Stewart, which was the name of a holding company that owned different businesses. They needed a director of communication.

The CEO evidently saw talent in me and he liked my style. He liked how I carried myself, how I spoke, and he wanted me to do advertising and marketing for his surgery centers.

It was an up-and-coming market. You could go in and a podiatrist would perform surgery on your foot or another might do a facelift. One day in, one day out, same place.

I worked with them for about two years and they paid me well. But it came to the point that I realized it wasn't for me. I hated waking up and going there each day. I just didn't like what I was doing.

I knew I was doing something right because I was financially successful and even able to finally afford my condo while putting money aside, but I wasn't happy with the work itself. At the magazine, I was always proud of my product. It was relevant, and I could have fun with it. In this new gig, I just didn't have that option and it made me feel unfulfilled.

I introduced a lot of different concepts, things I had learned during my time in sales, and my bosses were thrilled.

Deep down, however, I knew I wanted to get back into the media.

# Exercise Set 6:
# **Opportunities and Callings**

This exercise is designed focus you on the difference between taking openings versus opportunities. Gaining a sense of reflecting and understanding what fills your soul as much as what might fill your pocket book. One may be advantageous for the moment, but in the long run only your inner peace will matter.

First, what were your early career aspirations, and what do you think inspired that career?

_____

_____

_____


Have you ever felt like your true calling was somewhere other than where you were in the moment? Why?

_____

_____

_____

Have you ever seen someone succeed at something and thought: "I could do that if I really tried?" Name it and explain why.

_____

_____

_____

# 7.0
# **Facing Barriers**

P eople have asked me how to spot the flashes of opportunity and pitfalls life presents us. Is there a standard formula or answer within you that allows you to detect those moments and leverage them to your advantage?

The answer is going to be in the gut. I always trust my gut.

When I am forced to make decisions under pressure, I step back, close my eyes, and picture the moment and context of the decision I must make. Then, I act based on what feels right inside of me.

In order to trust in your gut reliably, you must first know and trust yourself. Those things don't come easily. It is all too simple to go through life without really knowing who you are—not understanding the potential that lies within you. We deceive ourselves about what we want and who we are because we often base our happiness in the expectations of others.

We want to make people we care about proud, so we become who they want us to be. In many cases, they don't want to hold you back. In fact, they feel they have your best interests at heart; but if you know, deep within yourself, that the path charted for you will not satisfy your basic drives, it may only lead you to frustration and unhappiness.

We have all been there. Everyone has been unhappy with the lot they have drawn. Necessity and survival, the struggle to maintain a basic hierarchy of needs: these all divert us from our destiny. Daily rituals can dampen our progress if we're not working toward it on our own time.

It is no wonder that some of the most successful and influential among us come from wealthy families. It is infinitely easier to focus the mind inward, especially during childhood, when worries are few and food is always on the table. For those who grow up under stressful circumstances, have experienced trauma, or lack stability, it can be harder to rise above. There's just more in your way.

However, even in the least hospitable places on our planet, life can thrive. Think of scorpions who live in the desert. For those who grew up fighting to survive, who come out stronger—they find their way to personal fulfillment through conquering adversity. Often, we find it is these most resilient people who rise to become incredible leaders.

And even for those with the privilege of basic securities, loving parents, and a supportive community, finding your truest, most trustworthy self is just plain hard. It is a negotiation between you and the world you're a part of at every moment. To set yourself on a path towards knowing yourself, you must trust yourself, maybe a self that hasn't fully emerged.

You must recognize the marvelous things that have happened in your life, and the difficult things which you overcame or were overwhelmed by.

You must trust that the Universe was made for kindness, caring, and beauty; and hold that trust so passionately within your soul that whatever decision you make, it will work itself out. You must discover the foresight which allows your inner self to know which decisions keep your success in reach.

When I make a tough decision, I trust that it will be right. I will, in spirit, compel the universe to bring it to fruition.

I fully believe I will be okay because I contribute to my own destiny.

## 7.1

# Blessings and Curses

F eeling dissatisfied in my role as a communication director because it shielded me from interacting with lots of different people, I decided it might be a good time to move on. I knew an open window would create an opportunity. Rusty, a friend who thought of me as a super salesman called to discuss starting a magazine together.

Rusty and I had been good friends at News Voice, and I always made sure to keep up with her over the years. She was a fashion illustrator and I used to have local stores send in their clothes for her to sketch.

She had a concept for a travel magazine she shared with me. I thought it was a great idea and suggested writing it in the first-person. She also offered that we distribute for free in Chicago. That's exactly what *the previous magazine did*. I thought bigger and suggested the *New York Times*.

I knew that the market for the *New York Times* would be ideal for a travel publication, and it was an instant qualifier for advertising. From that moment, we were a team creating *Travel My Way Magazine*.

I went to the local office for *The Times'* media sales and asked if we could distribute in the Sunday paper.

From that point, my life became infinitely more complicated. The magazine took off, but it created a period of stressors I had to find a way to overcome. There were great joys and great sadness's. And there are things I wish I had known then that have become clear years later in reflection.

Broadly speaking, when I was in my 20s, I hadn't faced a single lawsuit. I hadn't developed my first magazine until 29. In my 30s, I grew and sold a magazine that was largely my idea and successful because of my hard work. But, I was besieged with lawsuits and adversity. We all face our own terrible challenges.

The key is in learning from them.

## 7.2
# Actions and Reactions

Y our decisions in life bear not only on one person. By deciding to act in the world, you are choosing to change it, alter it for better or worse. Sometimes, we do things we think will create a better life for ourselves and the ones we love, but there are times when we do things out of impure motives. We treat others unfairly to preserve our status or simply because we have lost track of our own truth. The act becomes a negative force, dropped into the fabric of the Universe, rippling it like a gravitational wave.

I think *most* people in the world choose to act from a place of good. But, we can be horrified by the things people do to each other. Conversely, it can be hard to see when we're the one acting irrationally or causing harm to our own self.

I know that I have been crushed at things done to me over the years. Being teased when I was a young child because I was gay. I was used unfairly in the workforce because people wanted to hold me back. They created trickery to lure me off my path to success. Other times, I've found myself playing the trickster, acting from a place of fear.

As I've matured, I have realized that, when we treat others unjustly, there is always karmic payback. Most people learn early on that every action has an equal and complementary reaction, but we're hesitant to think of our actions in this world as having the same sway as a pendulum or a pool cue, transferring energy from your hand to a cue ball, to a cluster which clatters off every-which-way.

Of course, people aren't billiard balls, and it can take years to get accurate at predicting the outcome of our shots. After all, the Universe likes to put its own spin on things – but always for a reason.

We simply don't have the capacity to know all the logic of karmic reciprocity. It might not be a specific person we have wronged who's going to pay us back, and the opposing force may not return as strong. It might be years down the road, from a different avenue or completely different situation. The fact remains that, when you come from a place of ill intent, you will be responsible to deal with hardship in return.

Nothing goes unnoticed.

## 7.3

# Personal Responsibility

W hen unfortunate things have occurred in my life, I go back to my core and have faith that there is a reason I am being tested. That, if I stick with what I believe and follow the path I know I need to follow, then I will find my sunshine. I will find my day of peace.

We must take responsibility for our actions and recognize that we're constantly being affected by the choices of others. I believe we meet people who we've wronged in a past life, and, though we don't recognize them physically, we might encounter them based on some karmic payback. If you're paying attention, maybe you can see traces of that life here today.

Sometimes when bad things happen to me, I realize that it might be for something bad I did in a past life, and I just need to work through the situation. I need to deal with it, and I need to accept it. It's about stepping back and analyzing. Or it is a lesson to springboard me to something terrific in time, something I needed to learn now in order to move on to the next scene or act.

Not being reactionary but being responsive will get you out of your bind.

Often, I'll step back from a situation, take a deep breath, and ask myself if the problem will still bother me in 24 hours. Will it bother me in a week? Will it bother me in a few weeks?

If I find that it's going to bother me continuously through life, I need to find a way to address the situation. Weigh the decision of saying something to the person who is antagonizing me. If I witness a horrible injustice or cruelty and don't stand up: I can't protest. I don't have an option. All I can do is find the peace within myself and believe that, one day, the storm will end.

I often say, the sun will rise again, no matter how painful today was. After all, after every rain storm the sun does shine, it has for billions of years.

We too must rise above the occasion. We must train our spirits and souls to will greatness from the ashes of devastation and cruelty. We must believe, with strength, in our personal faiths and truths, while accepting the faith and truth of others, so that we might move forward.

Courage is nothing more than this: moving forward in the face of fear. Having the strength to weather the hard times, knowing it cannot last forever. The birth of spring follows the dead of winter, guaranteed.

## 7.4
# Disassembling Stress

Injustice and everyday life can induce stress and interfere with our ability to uncover our path. When I am stressed, I find decision making difficult, my motives skewed by outside adversity. I go to my core and I block everything out. Eventually, I realize that, rather than allowing moments to snowball, I must realize that situations and people who ask difficult things of me should not aggravate me: they're not really part of my stress.

I must be conscious to be kind and polite to all people and in every situation because that is who my true self is. I have to see past my stress to reach that place. Adversity and stress must be broken down and digested to do this in a healthy way.

A mouse can't eat a wedge of cheese whole: he needs to bite it into little pieces. That's what I do with my stress.

I compartmentalize and organize — How do I solve for this equation? What needs to be done first? — I get those things done. Then I begin to further diminish my list of stressors. Eventually, I find myself in a more comfortable place.

If I push stress aside, it only to comes back. And when it does, it is bigger or stronger.

I start at the root and work my way up. Like the roots of a tree, you must go deep within to realize how tall and strong you can stand. Sometimes your solutions work, but much like lab experiments, often something unexpected happens. And this result can be greater than your initial expectations. Sometimes when a "test" doesn't go as planned, if I can understand the cause, I'm offered yet another opportunity. No matter what the outcome, it's important I acted on my own hypothesis and tested it.

Sometimes your solutions work, but, much like in a laboratory experiments sometimes something unexpected happens. Sometimes your work leads to something greater. Sometimes when a solution doesn't go as planned, if I can understand the cause, I'm offered an opportunity to conclude I would have never come to before. No matter the outcome, it is important that I acted on my hypothesis and tested it.

This approach underscores the importance of being a responsive person as opposed to a reactionary person. When I get very aggravated or heated in a moment, in a situation, or I find somebody is pulling me back, I respond after I've had time to contemplate. I believe people are like mirrors, our actions reflected off others. There's no point in being reactionary. It makes no sense to create conflict among people if my goal is to create a calm productive environment around myself.

# Exercise Set 7:
# **Facing Barriers**

This exercise set is designed to reveal the negative forces or actors in your life so that they can be acknowledged and addressed, creating an opportunity to respond rather than react. As you identify these forces, we're reminded that there is also positivity in our lives and focusing there can pull us forward...

So, first off, what are some negative forces in your life?

_____

_____

_____

How do you address them?

_____

_____

_____

How have you overcome dark times?

_____

_____

_____

Think about a person your feel positive around, what does that energy feel like?

_____

_____

_____

## 8.0

# Greatness Through Connectedness

G reatness and success aren't measured by an objective level or scale. Greatness is more like a metaphor. It makes us smile. It makes us zealous. It makes us joyful. It gives us bursts of energy to do other things. It makes our hearts feel warm and fuzzy. It is cozy. It is comfortable.

Imagine a scale of greatness and make it a 12-inch ruler. Think of the most joyous accounts of our life as the 12-inch mark, and our lowest moments at the other end. We can use this ruler to reflect, training our minds to reflect on joyous times no matter where we are at the present.

Our future successes, our future greatness, our futures in general, are informed by our past, and our past lives. Remembering to dwell on the best within us brings all that positive energy closer to us, helping us achieve the same in the present, and the future.

Ultimately, we must use our positive energies, contained within memories, to tide us over through the dark times—perhaps to even hasten their departure. It's easy for us to fall into the sinister traps of darkness, however. It's so easy for us to succumb, and I think it is for a multitude of reasons. One major one would be that we are conditioned to think negatively. All too often, that is the message of the world. Even the most sheltered and privileged among us face hardships and tragedy. For some, the world is immeasurably more stressful and tragic.

Parents leave or mistreat their families. Siblings and friends take paths which lead to addiction or economic hardship. Negative people sour our thoughts of humanity. We see countries torn apart by greed and selfishness. If extraterrestrial life happened to be tuning in to a newscast, they might determine our species to be one of violence and hate.

It becomes a mindset. You start to think everything is bad—all the time. A little cynicism is fine, but when you get to thinking it's all gone down the tubes, it's not a good thing.
It can't be a good thing.

People are sometimes negative because they're too afraid to be positive. Remember fear is just faith turned inside-out and people learn to be afraid of good things, thinking 'good' shouldn't happen to them at all. They don't feel they're special inside. They don't feel good about themselves. Perhaps they lack self-esteem or crave attention.

In any case, it becomes easy for them to think everything is bad, because if the world is inherently evil in their personal truth, they won't be further disappointed if things don't work out the way they want.

People also become negative when they attempt to succeed, and success does not come. They give up. They quit the race just before the finish line. They commit to believing that they cannot push themselves to go any further. They can't energize themselves, and nobody is motivating or pushing them, so they just stop.

But the secret is, just before you're ready to quit, you give it one more shot beyond your breaking point, that's when you win. This process is called the "extra-ordinary motion," which creates that extraordinary moment.

When I see someone in need of help—someone in that kind of dark and feral place—I try to do what I can. Sometimes, it is a dollar or a bowl of chicken soup, but more often that's the lazy answer. Sometimes, it is a kind word and the company of a friend. I try to entrust my positive energy to those I meet.

I offer my time and support to those who even seem incapable of helping themselves due to negativity, or circumstance of birth benefit—especially them, because they struggle every day to survive.

We don't have a complete instruction manual for the human brain. We don't know how to raise our children perfectly, every time. We have experts, today, who tell us what is best, perhaps, more than 99% of the time. Yet, our greater knowledge is incomplete. As we learn, everything is trial and error. We learn from each other. We are each other's instruction manual.

We experiment with life and with our actions. We seed the world with every choice, and every choice grows, new generations spawning from that singular human intention. Sometimes, our experiments don't work out, but sometimes they defy our wildest dreams. That means, we need to keep striving. Continue experimenting! Seriously, now is a decent time to put down the book and start thinking, because you may just be putting the same energy into the universe every day. Like I am at times, you may be a person of habit and routine right now.

When did you stop doing the things you love? —the you-ness of the world you've been missing all these years.

This is it. It has never left you. And all you have to do is listen and try.

Try summoning new energies into your reality. Take up a new hobby. Learn to cook a new dish. Learn to cook if you don't know already! Binge watch Sense8 with your cousins from Ohio. Try a new cuisine or try on a new jacket. Just a little bit of change can make it all come together. How, you might ask? Simply by introducing something new into your routine produces a chain reaction creating an artery of opportunity – a new energy source! Maybe your new hobby will introduce you to Mr. or Ms. Right, a new career path, new friend and so on. Because you've gone from routine to protein, adding something healthy to your daily mix and we know protein helps us grow.

If we learn, equally, from our failures and successes, then, maybe, we can learn to modify certain things within us, or modify how we approach future situations.

Granted, some people need extra help, but, if everyone could reframe their minds and think about the fact that, from the most negative times, we can create positive ones.

Two negatives can make a positive in physics — why not in life?

# 8.1

# **Re-Defining the Negative**

D aily life presents us with all kinds of people, but I'm going to share with you three kinds of people we interact with who are particularly challenging. I want to offer the wisdom to detect who they are, and how to confront their worldview in a way that will make life easier for you personally, but also enlighten them with a new ideology.

The three groups we'll address here are negative people, non-trusting people, and non-directional people.

Negative people, naturally, are their own worst enemy. They believe everything is bad, nothing is going to work out—it can't happen, it won't happen—they're naysayers. They often live sad lives, not realizing that they have imprisoned their minds within their own trap. They think they are alone and singular in their struggle. They don't understand faith, they don't believe in a greater good. They are lost in life.

When I meet these people, I find that I have to almost reset their thinking. I must gain their trust, so they feel comfortable enough to believe that things—*or at least one thing*—will work out and that not everyone is trying to rip them off. You must use both psychology and factual data to work through these types of people.

You must earn trust, so their negative behavior can be countered with positive. What's interesting here, is that when they finish their time with me, some fall back into their negative behavior, but some are at a point within their lives when they can begin to rethink their worldview. In some cases, I can provide a link or an off-ramp to a new route.

Non-trusting people are like the popular conception of a control freak. They don't trust people. It's possible that, during the course of their lives they have had tragic things happen to them that have prompted them to try to control their situations completely. By closing themselves off to the possibility of outside change, they don't have to worry so much about a loss of anything that they would find to be of conflict, or misfortune.

These untrusting or controlling people tend to also think they're better at whatever anyone else is doing. They often do know a lot, they just don't want to believe the person they're working with really knows what they're doing. These people can also make you feel like you're inferior in light of their superiority. They make you believe that whatever they think is right is right. They want you to do things their way, not the way your expertise would know.

I deal with many people in real estate who think they know pricing models better than I do, or they know how to negotiate this emotional transaction than I do. Sometimes they do, but most of the time it feels as if they are coming from a place of insecurity. I've even been there as a young person. I remember feeling like I could do my manager's job better than they could—the truth is, back then, I probably couldn't have— but I never acted on my ambitions. I did my job and didn't step on any toes.

Be careful of the toes you step on today. They may be connected to the ass you kiss tomorrow. Life isn't a mystery all the time. Karma often creates a through-line we can follow quite easily.

Not everyone is quite so easy on their presumptions of expertise though. My way of working with these people is to explain to them the numbers: I've been the top 1% performing broker in my market since 2007, which means I've sold hundreds and hundreds of properties— they may have sold 2, 5, 10?

I establish credibility immediately so there is no questioning my method. Establishing credibility is always the first step when working with these kinds of people. When they start to become non-trusting, or controlling, reminding them of your ability to deliver is a great way to get them off their track, and move them onto yours.

Our third and final persona includes the undefined, negative people who are lost. They simply don't have a place from which to begin. They are afraid. They may not necessarily be negative, but they are non-committal. They want something, but they don't know how to obtain it or even what it is. They don't know how to organize what they want into an actionable thought.

In some cases, these people find their lives feel empty. And because they're disorganized and non-committal, they are confined to drifting in the moment, living day-to-day like a mouse wandering a maze. If they hit a brick wall, they'll go in a different direction. Maybe something will come to them this way, but they are severely cutting their odds of success by relying on undirected trial and error. (Consciously informed trial and error is something entirely different, of course.)

These undefined people are challenging, because, like a vinyl record, you have to cue them up. You must set them on a path and put them back when they start looping the same ideas over and over again. To make a noticeable change in their life, you must find what drives them, what they most desire: their little wedge of cheese.

You must take the cheese from the mouse and break it into smaller pieces for them—digestible goals they can meet. Those smaller pieces will go down easy and they will be ready for more. Hopefully, they will realize that the cheese is leading them in a specific direction.

When you provide them the steps or the staircase, they will know to take one step at a time. They may even begin challenging themselves to achieve the next level. Once you set them on the right course and begin to focus their minds, in many cases they can begin learning how to see themselves in the future.

## 8.2

# Guiding Language

When it comes to working with negative and unguided people as a real estate agent, you try to get them to figure out what they want. You take them through an assessment program: pulling out specifics of what they might be looking for.

In short, you need to dig and ask them questions.

There needs to be a teacher-student learning process, where copious questioning helps define a process. Then you need to schedule them, regulate them, so that they can go with the flow and, together, we can all find what's best for them.

From your initial guidance, you must continue your instruction, in some capacity, by establishing a code or language, behavioral triggers to exchange with each other. When those of us who are already positive are looking for people to align with, these are the cues we look for. To bring positivity to those who are less guided, or more negative, they have to draw it in themselves.

For people who are already positive, it's almost like a secret handshake, but one we don't think about very much. And what comes naturally to us, may prove to be entirely more complicated to someone who has spent their life in a negative space.

I believe that the choices people make propel them towards those presenting similar energies in the Universe. Actions, positive and negative, are how we communicate.

And behavioral patterns—the learned way in which we string actions together—becomes like a cultural dialect, spoken most fluently by those who have the same behaviors.

Actions which will draw positive people to you have a lot to do with how you treat other people. It's letting somebody sneak in when you're in a line of cars. It's speaking kindly to a cashier at a checkout stand. It's telling somebody you love them. It's putting somebody else's needs in front of your own—not literally or metaphorically speaking—it's simple acts of actual unselfishness.

Imagine you're raising money for a charity or assisting elderly people or sharing your enthusiasm for what you're doing with friends. That's positivity. That is something that is helping humanity. That is trying to inspire other people through your actions. That's how we find validation and bring it to others.

Most importantly, when you meet others' energies head on with our own confidence and positive outlook, we win them over almost every time. Acts of kindness, those golden threads that illuminate your tapestry of life, develop your competitive edge toward the light of success.

# 8.3

# **Positive Force**

S ometimes, even the most positive people have negative moments. You find positive people everywhere who are in a hurry, shedding their positivity in a moment of exasperation. They'll block people from the on-ramp when traffic is heavy. They become mired in the monotony of getting to where they need to go and forget the lives of others.

This just shows us how important remaining positive is. Because even the most positive among us can lose that outlook so easily. It's a fragile gift! And many people only know how to hold their delicate peace so carefully. Just a small shake up in their lives can momentarily shatter their entire mindset.

Luckily, all of us are capable of bringing positivity into our lives. And we all have fluctuations of behavioral traits so, just because you break your cool one day, doesn't mean you can't repair it the next. As I've said before, the sun will come up tomorrow, and, if you let it, the new day will gift you with a new, measured mindset.

In the moment, we are one person, reacting to events occurring around us. In the next moment, we are someone completely different. Because we are constantly changing, and the world is constantly changing around us, I think that we must look at the overall consistency of somebody's behavior rather than one action or two actions. It's not fair to discount somebody based on one experience, but in too many cases we'll do it. We'll talk about these people by saying, "They're not a positive person."

The truth is: we are all human. We all make mistakes. We weren't born with instruction manuals. There is no such thing as perfection in the absolute. There is no such thing as perfection in humankind or in nature. We have conjoined twins. We have double-budded roses. We have things that occur, which seem unpleasant to some, but there is a beauty there that we just don't sometimes recognize.

Perhaps these irregularities in the fabric of life are there to teach others a lesson. I sometimes wonder if conjoined twins are here to teach the rest of us a lesson. Maybe, because they're connected in this life, the people around them are supposed to learn something from their existence. Maybe they are two people tied together, who need to learn something truly profound from one another in this life.

From a difficult situation and seeming irregularities in our lives can come some wonderful things. We look at somebody like Helen Keller, who was born deaf, blind and mute, struggling to find her place in the world, but through hard work and unrelenting passion expressed by those around her, she became a positive force for all of humanity.

*Security is mostly a superstition. It does not exist in nature nor do the children of man experience it as a whole. Life is either a daring adventure or nothing.*

*--H. Keller*

# Exercise Set 8:
# **Meaningful Connections**

In this exercise set, we work to identify the things that connect us to one another and the world around us. Identifying these connections helps us realize how much more there is to each of us than our individual self. It also helps strengthen our understanding that each action we take undergoes a multiplying affect in the world... so we must stay focused on doing good by all.

First off, have you ever felt connected to a greater whole? When?

_____

_____

_____

What type of people do you think are drawn to you?

_____

_____

_____

What does your best self-look like to others?

_____

_____

_____


How can you bring that best self-more fully into the
world?

_____

_____

_____

# 9.0
# **Growth**

I nteraction goes deep, and the wires between karmic events become difficult to trace. All we know is that we create positive stimuli in the world, and it sets the universe on a positive spin.

Beautiful rainbows emerge from terrible rainstorms. We gaze upon the stars and feel a deep joy. When people decide to perform an act of kindness, they feel this same joy. That joy creates energy, and that energy flows through the universe: it connects people from all walks of life—a tapestry of sorts.

It is the same feeling we get when we participate in something greater than ourselves: a live music event where everyone feels the same rhythm—dancing to the same beat; a speech which moves your passions; a book which makes you question and redefine your role in the world; a ceremony whereby one achieves a higher status.

Social scientists call this feeling, "collective effervescence," a non- verbal connection between people participating in the same event. I call it, "That feeling in my soul that feels like home."

But, as we've established, not everyone is cued into the language of the Universe to the same degree. We don't all have the same upbringing or the same educational experiences which ultimately allow us to recognize the signs in the stars and the energies all around.

Even though we all come with unique strengths and sensitivities, we're also only as strong as our weakest link. We're just one big chain, and when one person acts, it touches someone else who is connected to someone else and so on. We have a stadium and beyond of energy, a plane of consciousness where things just continue to perpetuate into greatness.

It's almost like a chain letter that instructs the recipient to pass it on to 10 people. Yes, they can be quite annoying, but the fact is that at the core you want this lovely letter, your actions, your words, to touch another life.

The negativity of course of those letters is when they threaten you. They say, "If you don't do this within the next hour, you'll have misfortune." It became almost like a religious duty, like telling somebody, if you don't do this—if you sin—you'll go to hell. And yet, we can live in heaven or hell, right here on earth, depending on our chosen mindset.

But our actions aren't like this when they're positive: there is no threat or string attached when positive acts are pure. If there's no expectation for gain, then the good and the pureness continues to fold into the world: one life after another.

But, all too often, people think their positive behaviors should be repaid with great expectations or demands. When that is the case, then the action can only be like a firecracker: it's going to have a very short fuse and it might impact one or two or three or four or a million people, only to fizzle out quickly. There's no growth pattern to that type of behavior. It is simply not sustainable.

# 9.1
# **Personal Truth**

S o where does your personal truth fit into this equation of reciprocal forces and laws of attraction? What does your inner belief have to do with any of this? How will it guide you to success in whatever field you choose? Is it a religious commitment or just another language we must learn how to speak?

And what about past lives? You didn't think this real estate broker would be talking about reincarnation, did you?

Well here are the answers, or at least the answers as far as I've discovered.

We walk down the street in this life carrying the weight of the many lives before us. They tug at our perceptions and decision-making processes. They impose themselves into our personal truth. Our past lives are messengers of lessons learned long ago, in another body.

And this is where we return to keeping your senses tuned-in to the subtle signs of the Universe. Walking down the street, a thought pops into your head. You think little of it, but later realize it was a communication from perhaps another life: a sign from the Universe, a signal of sorts.

In some cases, it's as if we're blind. We'll meet someone who feels particularly familiar and we connect. We need to remember to acknowledge the people and things we have known before. All too often, they are the harbingers of great change—for better or worse. In many cases, you have known a person you are meeting now in previous experience forever. You recognize their energy and connect to that. Their current face is unfamiliar.

If we are tuned-in, then we can more easily achieve greatness, by some standard. If you have a sense to wait to leave a room, wait. If you have a sense to turn left instead of your planned right, turn right. Our senses can open us to reconnect to the past and therefore what is most important to us now. We listen to gain the upper hand by keeping ourselves open to these forces. They springboard us to spectacular places.

And when something changes for the better, when we take one more step towards our goals, we must be grateful for the gift that brought us there and pass it along to others. Because goodness is real. Goodness is truthful. Goodness is a connection.

We could relate this to the Taoist theory of nature. We juxtapose the bareness and cold of winter with the delight of snowy blankets covering the ground. All of it is necessary to help bacteria decompose old roots and organic matter. It is necessary to fertilize the soil and replenish groundwater. It prepares the ground for tulips and grass, vegetables and birth, and everything else that comes with the beauty of spring... everything that allows us to sustain life.

With people, we need that full-time connection, or a semblance of one. We need to keep our promises to maintain our connection with goodness and we will inspire our peers to elevate and enable others to do great things.

Whether we dedicate our day or our life to noble causes, whether we touch another life and help them succeed, we reveal our essences. And our essences are angelic.

We can even help people attain greatness in their lives. Since we all come from the same source—the Universe—we are all connected. So too are our gifts and destinies. By becoming all you can be, by taking the correct path to get there, you pull up others around you into this more comforting light.

Our crowning achievements, our fulfillment of personal destinies, bring us closer to what religious people would call God. For people who don't recognize religion, but believe in a greater good, it's positive energy. And that energy source, that faith in God, is all the same source of boundless goodness.

Think about this. There is no reason for the source of goodness and love to harbor us in hell. Fear can imprison us, while love wraps us in a sense of security that we are safe.

Best of all, we carry pieces of this energy with us everywhere we go!

# 9.2
# **Attributes**

The greater good in the Universe may be a boundless energy accessible to everyone, but that doesn't mean it is a simple equation to decipher. Fulfilling your destiny is a lifetime pursuit and reaching your potential will not happen quickly.

Mozart may have been a prodigy, but he didn't compose for just a few moments—he spent his entire—though rather short—lifetime working on his music. Creative forces dwell within us and wrestle themselves out before they emerge fully. It's just like the seed we planted several chapters ago: it will eventually grow, but it must be tended and cared for over time with the help of others if possible.

And your greater goodness, your personal destiny and truth is not a singular force either. There are a cadre of attributes which may be tested and developed to get to this place of attainment. Before you can go out and accomplish that, you must learn the details.

From my perspective, I'll share some attributes I believe make me, and could make you, a successful real estate broker.

I think everyone is capable of learning any kind of an occupation to a large degree, but clearly, there's a lot more at play than simple knowledge of real estate and its technicalities, though that is certainly some of it. The "formulas" of real estate are easily learned, but there are aspects that some of us are not capable of learning. Some of us don't even have interest in learning them.

For instance, I understand accounting to some degree, but I have no interest in being an accountant— it's not my specialty—and, even if I had completed some academic coursework, I would probably struggle to push myself in the field, because I have no real interest in it.

Some people, because of their chosen journey, come later to the discovery of their desires. If you decide you want to calculate rocket trajectories after going to school for a legal career, you may have a longer road of complicated equations than you would have otherwise. But, that base knowledge will help you be successful because it is these base skills which ultimately makes our accomplishments effortless.

My profession *is* real estate, and in real estate, it is vital to have self- confidence and know how to display it without looking arrogant. Your client feeds off and benefits from your confidence. It's confidence that makes others feel safe and secure. They want to know that you are going to be able to help them with what could be the largest transaction they will make in their lifetime. Your first action is to sell yourself, sell your trust, and then trust in your client to reciprocate that trust in you as an asset. It's wildly simple and incredibly complicated.

A genuine and congenial personality is a good place to start. You have to make people feel cared for. You have to make people feel you are their most trusted advisor who will be there through every step and turn. You also must make sure that they have a hunger to succeed.

They need a burning desire within themselves to go through this process, because, when they're done with one transaction, they will have to move on to the next. So, will you. And the sooner you do, the better for both parties. So, you must sew that importance into the relationship from day one.

You must push and forge ahead to make your way as an agent. You must understand situations so, if something does arise, you are on it already. Finally, you must prepare your client to reflect positivity back to the world. You need referrals to survive, and the only way to earn a good referral is to perform to the best of your ability every single day.

An eagerness to please can also be a boon to your success. I see that as a common theme among brokers: they want to make people feel good, they want to please their clients. But *extra-ordinary* brokers want to go to the ends of the earth to make clients feel like the most important person. Everyone wants to feel like they're going to get all the attention that's required to successfully complete their mission.

Finding compatible personalities to work with also helps. It's interesting to see how we match with other people: where one personality works best with certain personalities. We all have our presences. Timid people might not feel comfortable with someone whose personality is more aggressive.

Personalities need to match in order to work well together, but as an agent, you are the one who is ultimately responsible for making the client feel welcomed and comfortable. For someone who is quieter, you have to work beyond that trait and find where their strengths lie. After all, you are partaking on a mission together. You need to play off your own unique skills and experiences.

A successful salesperson, then, should be able to meet their audience where they are and speak in a voice and act in a manner they would expect. We mirror ourselves to acclimate to others. To me, that's really the number one attribute of a successful person in real estate and really in any sales business. You need to know your basics, but you also need to be able to mold, model and showcase yourself as the parallel personality of the person (or people) you're working with to reveal what can be born.

You need to know when to dress up or dress down; know, mentally how to be energetic or more reserved; know how to speak to someone in a certain manner or hold your tongue. When you model yourself on the person that you're serving, you make them the central focus and gain a deeper understanding of their wants and needs.

## 9.3
# The Power of Attitude

One final attribute I'd like to draw attention to as a universally salient concept is simply this: attitude.

An unwavering, can-do attitude is one of the most valuable tools at your disposal. If you believe it, it is so much more likely to work out. And that, I believe, is the attribute which ultimately separates successful people from less the successful (bearing in mind, 'success' is not purely define in monetary terms).

Belief in the ability of a problem to be solved is the first step to learn somebody else's language. If you're positive and believe things will work out and bring that attitude when you communicate, you'll draw people to you. You'll reel in the brightness of success through physical and non-verbal choices.

Make yourself the reason your clients' eyes glow. The eyes, they say, are the window to the soul. Learn how your clients carry themselves, how they react to things. Again, find the joy and care they see in their actions and be responsive when something doesn't go right.

Ultimately, the determining factor of a positive person will always come back to attitude. As long as I am true to my word and follow through with what I say, making it a point to hold my truth in the highest regard.

A positive person's word is their bond.

And that is what draws positive people together.

They're explorers, but explorers need a community of like-minded people who can be trusted.

Positive people explore the unknown, and to probe the unknown, you have to discover who you are first.

They move forward in the face of adversity, believing that no matter what challenges life presents them, whatever tasks must be completed, they will continue with their goal. Positive people don't encounter road blocks—they only face obstacles they can learn from and will ultimately overcome.

# Exercise Set 9:
# **Directed Growth**

This exercise set is all about gaining an understanding of how you evolve in the context of who you are in the world around you. Growing your career or simply improving your personal outlook all comes from the same place... an acknowledgement of where you are and responding with the tools you have available.

First, list two or three examples when you were closed to change.

_____

_____

_____

Why were you opposed to the changes in your examples?

_____

_____

_____

Look back at the three sentences you used to describe yourself in. Within this context, would you still describe yourself this way?

_____

_____

_____

Now list two or three examples when you embraced a change.

_____

_____

_____

Why were you able to lean into the changes listed?

_____

_____

_____

Look back at Exercise Set One again. Is this more in line with how you described yourself?

_____

_____

_____

# 10.0
# **Sustaining**

We talk about leading by example, and I think that's how positive people travel through their lives. Their overall behavior and actions are consistent with helping others achieve their goals. They give love. They give advice. When they see a coin on the ground, they'll turn it from heads to tails and make a wish so the next person who discovers it can make *their* wish come true. They open doors for elderly people, for people who are laden with parcels, for people—no matter who they are. When they get on an elevator, they say hello or wish someone a nice day on the way out.

Those small acts of kindness become part of your larger kindnesses. Just keep passing that kindness on. Keep doing things without expecting to get something in return. No agenda is needed. Be pure, because you can see pureness in how others carry themselves, and they can see it in you.

We can't just pass by other's display of kindness and positivity. To give them power, we must bear witness to those healthy exchanges around us. An act of positivity I recently witnessed involved a young lady at Starbucks.

As she exited the storefront, I saw her pass a man sitting on the street begging for money. She turned around and went back to the man. I was stopped at a red light just looking around when I saw her give him some money and begin to chat with him. Of course, I had no idea what they said, but I noticed that when she left his company, the man had developed a smile on his face.

That was a powerful moment for me to witness because it spoke to the necessity of acts of kindness in our lives, how positivity in one person can be reflected, perhaps, onto somebody else.

That one interaction might not dig the homeless man out of poverty, but maybe the positive spark passed from the woman onto him might cause a small change in his daily experience. How many other times will the same beggar be passed over and overlooked? How many people will simply choose to look away? Certainly, more than those who will give him a dollar or a kind word. What if that weren't the case?

Those few moments of love and care might stick with him in a strong way. He might think differently because of that interaction. Maybe, he'll pass on the positivity by helping another homeless person. Maybe the woman who helped him out will go to work and have something fortunate happen to her. Maybe she'll get a raise. Maybe she'll have nothing happen to her. Maybe she'll get a phone call from somebody she hasn't heard from in years.

No matter what the case, it is easier to think positively than negatively, as it keeps the mind more fluid for your dreams to come true.

# 10.1
# Darkness

E veryone has times where we enter places of darkness: places of anxiety where life's uncertainty touches our daily lives and ventures. Things we're planning to get to become hard. You feel low, disenchanted with relationships and everything else.

I remember after selling 80% of Travel Your Way magazine to a large corporation who made promises to grow the circulation to 4 million and invest all their resources to make it a huge success; they rescinded on their promises and sent me on my way with nothing except the intellectual property.

Devastated and lonely, I spent a year trying to regroup and figure out the next chapter of my life. I took the time to reflect on what I had done in create this situation. I came to realize two things: first, I lost my true self by believing that having money would make me happy and, secondly, that tall, dark and handsome was the answer to my dream. What I changed was my thought process. On the subject of the magazine, I knew that I had to create a more current concept for the marketplace and on the subject of love I had to stop looking for the physical attributes and focus on the spiritual. I identified the three things that I dream for in a person: 1) someone to make me laugh as much as I returned the same. 2) someone to inspire me as much as I returned the same. 3) someone to love me as much as I returned the same. Perhaps you think this is to idealistic and maybe to most people it is but to me, a person who pins themselves to hope, well, I knew if I put it out to the universe and stuck with it- it would happen for me. Long story short- for more than a year I felt like a yoyo- there were lots of ups and downs, but I trusted myself not to waiver in my belief. Eventually, I can honestly say, both my personal and professional lives changed remarkably.

I think that when we have these negative periods in our lives, they have the potential to be the beginning of a fabulous new chapter in your journey. It doesn't happen right away. Any major change takes time... takes time to germinate.

It's not an immediate, "Wow. It's dark tonight and tomorrow the sun will come out." It could be dark for months. It could be dark for years. Then, suddenly, it can become bright.

It's like putting a seed into the ground. It doesn't become a plant overnight. It must break the seed casing and reach out green tendrils. It must be nurtured, whether by a farmer or by nature itself. Then it can grow. And it grows wild, at its own pace so it can absorb all the proper nutrients, eventually becoming a stem. That is the natural progression of life, of nature, and of the sun.

We must sew positivity into our very deepest truths so that, when these dark times come, we can look at our seedlings—tender moments, people we are close to—and remember how much we have taken upon ourselves. How many lives rely on our own actions and how those actions will affect the tiny hints of life when the darkness has passed.

It's the course of the night to become day. The rainstorm will end. The sun will come out. We have negative moments in our lives. We face anxiety-provoking situations. We will always get through them, because we reflect on other times when we might have had similar feelings or periods of darkness followed by triumph.

How we deal with our moments of darkness frames our minds to seek happy thoughts, positive moments within the history of our life. We naturally reflect on good times, greatness, happiness, and joy.

We say, "We have happiness and we'll have it again." That is the cyclical way of the Universe and we must accept it.

# 10.2
# **Staying Open**

I was still in my rut in an old job when Stephen, my partner, said to me, "Look, you really have a great eye for design and you love houses."

We had just bought a place and flipped it. And it was true: I had always loved houses. I remember when I was younger I always used to love to go into houses and look at them. I remember when I was in college I used to sometimes go to Sunday open houses just to look.

I must have had something incubating with real estate.

So, Stephen encouraged me to go into real estate. I tested for my real estate license and I thought I might as well just go for the top dog license: a managing broker's license. It's more course work, but I did it. I did the classes. I crammed it all into a week and then I tested.

I got my license. That was in 2002.

At that point we were selling our loft in River North because we were building a row house in in the same neighborhood.

Now if you're thinking, Michael, where the hell did the money for that come from?" I'd be honest: I didn't have any money, but I did have some money.

I had a little saved and, of course, Stephen had a great job. We were just able to do it within budget. Whether or not we had any money is beside the point though. The long and short of this situation is that I started in real estate.

First a friend couldn't find a broker. She asked for my help. She'd heard that Stephen and I had done well with our property flipping endeavors and wanted us to do the same for her. I feel silly saying it now, but at the time I told her, "I don't do that for the public." Imagine being basically without a job and someone asks you to do something you enjoy for a little extra money and declining!

Well, she told me she thought I would be an excellent broker and that she and her husband needed his help. A friend in need tends to need you. And I can't help but help a friend, so I did it. I helped them find a place. One thing led to another and my real estate career began.

I remember sending out the word to some of my close friends. I got a call from someone who asked me to sell his house. I told him I was just starting out. I wasn't sure if I had the experience he wanted.

My friend said, "It's okay. What you don't know about real estate you make up for just your creative knowledge. You're honorable and you're ethical and you always do what you say."

And that's what's led me to today. And today I can say that I will still turn down a job if I don't think I'm the right person. And my word is still my bond. I don't make promises I know I can't keep.

Since starting my career in real estate, I've had the pleasure of bringing countless families a new life, or a renewed sense of relief that the details of one of the most major transactions they'll ever make are in the hands of someone who truly devotes himself entirely to his customers.

For me, this devotion to the work I do and the people I make commitments to has been my hallmark. No matter where my path leads me next, I know that knowledge will bring me (and you!) a sense of purpose and belonging.

# Exercise Set 10:
# **Sustaining Growth**

Our final exercise set focuses on taking the work we've done so far and putting into perpetual motion. Of course, we're not done here. Once you complete this exercise, pull everything together and review it in total. You'll find, to some degree, you've probably written a book like this one—probably even a better one. I'd welcome you to share it with your friends, share it with me, share it with the world. You are constantly becoming and improving and changing and that alone can inspire the world. Here we go...!

First, make a list of two to three things that inspire you.

_____

_____

_____

What does your list reveal to you?

_____

_____

_____

How will you use these wonderful things that inspire you to embrace the changes ahead and life's greater plan for you?

_____

_____

_____


What will be your cues be for you to return to your inspirations?

_____

_____

_____

# 11.0
# **Segue**

I n our work together, I've told you a little about my ideas and myself. We've talked a lot about my personal truth and how I came to the place in my life I am today.

*Notice, this final portion of our book is not a 'conclusion!'*

I can't stress enough how important some of these lessons I have learned can be. It is absolutely essential to live every day by the standards of your personal truth. And, even more essentially, to allow your truth to develop and evolve as you take in more experiences on life's path.

When you unlock your truth and live by it, you also unlock gifts; you rediscover passions and talents; you learn how to share and reciprocate. From here, you may find yourself coming more and more to a place of reflection. Find yourself there in the moment. Leverage your past to inform your future. Pay attention to the cyclical signs that reveal themselves around us.

By reflecting and questioning and discovering, you will find yourself with decisions or at odds with a force of adversity. This is a part of growth and change. You may even find yourself in a state of distress for long periods of time. Even in these darkest of times, we must all persevere with positivity and compassion. The sun will never stop rising.

Eventually, we learn to read the signs of the Universe with fluency. We become less confined by our choices. We discover new possibilities, new challenges, and we face them. By this method, we will achieve greatness and success. We will become our fullest selves and maybe even glimpse the fringe of what we know to be true.

Finally, I showed you manifestations of my method which have reveled themselves in my life. I waxed nostalgic on what makes me successful at what I do. But maybe real estate isn't your thing. You are the only one who knows. Others are always there to help you find your way.

Self-Discovery is a constant and eternal process which we will never complete. All we can do is hold on to our beliefs and dreams in the hope that they will bring us to the places we want to go. We also have to fight and struggle every day to make these things happen in our lives, but that is how we evolve. It is the protein which makes us stronger. Remember that a wave in the ocean eventually crashes, but it always rises again.

For me, I am happy to bring the joy of homeownership to people from all walks of life. I do everything I can to help minimize the anxiety of every little detail. It's where I've come to feel fulfilled in what I do, while also utilizing things I'm good at.

You could say I'm happy.

And that happiness is what we're all kind of looking for, I guess. Please tell me if you disagree. And that's why we're here today, because I want you to be happy and successful. It is your inherent right.

I think that anybody can be open to messaging about positive thought. I think it can work for marketing people, PR people. It can work for fashion people, it can work for salespeople, it can work for firefighters, police officers, and yes, even politicians. I think it basically is a platform to be able to help people navigate their lives and find that connection to truth that lies deep within themselves.

It's that deep belief and having that faith that things will always work out—that you meet people at certain times because it's a connection that will perhaps lead you to a better place down the road in your journey of life.

There are no accidents, and nothing happens by mistake... because we all deserve to live happily ever ~~after~~ - *always!*